cajun

cajun

THE AUTHENTIC TASTE OF SPICY LOUISIANA COOKING

foreword by
ruby le bois

southwater

This edition is published by Southwater
Southwater is an imprint of Anness Publishing Ltd
Hermes House, 88–89 Blackfriars Road, London SE1 8HA
tel. 020 7401 2077; fax 020 7633 9499
www.southwaterbooks.com; info@anness.com
© Anness Publishing Ltd 1996, 2004

UK agent: The Manning Partnership Ltd, 6 The Old Dairy, Melcombe Road, Bath BA2 3LR; tel. 01225 478444; fax 01225 478440;
sales@manning-partnership.co.uk
UK distributor: Grantham Book Services Ltd, Isaac Newton Way, Alma Park Industrial Estate, Grantham, Lincs NG31 9SD; tel. 01476 541080; fax
01476 541061; orders@gbs.tbs-ltd.co.uk
North American agent/distributor: National Book Network, 4501 Forbes Boulevard, Suite 200, Lanham, MD 20706; tel. 301 459 3366;
fax 301 429 5746; www.nbnbooks.com
Australian agent/distributor: Pan Macmillan Australia, Level 18, St Martins Tower, 31 Market St, Sydney, NSW 2000; tel. 1300 135 113;
fax 1300 135 103; customer.service@macmillan.com.au
New Zealand agent/distributor: David Bateman Ltd, 30 Tarndale Grove, Off Bush Road, Albany, Auckland; tel. (09) 415 7664; fax (09) 415 8892

A CIP catalogue record for this book is available from the British Library.

Publisher Joanna Lorenz
Senior Cookery Editor Linda Fraser
In-house Editor Anne Hildyard
Designer Nigel Partridge
Illustrations Madeleine David
Photographers Edward Allwright, Steve Baxter, James Duncan and Amanda Heywood
Recipes Carla Capalbo, Sarah Gates, Ruby Le Bois, Laura Washburn and Steven Wheeler
Food for photography Jane Hartshorn, Elizabeth Wolf-Cohen and Wendy Lee
Stylists Hilary Guy and Blake Minton
Cover Photography Nicki Dowey, *Food Stylist* Emma Patmore, *Design* Wilson Harvey

Previously published as part of the *Classic* cookery series

Typeset by MC Typeset Ltd, Rochester, Kent

1 3 5 7 9 10 8 6 4 2

For all recipes, quantities are given in both metric and imperial measures, and, where appropriate, measures are also given in
standard cups and spoons. Follow one set, but not a mixture, because they are not interchangeable.

Picture on frontispiece and pages 7, 8 and 9: Zefa Pictures Ltd.

CONTENTS

FOREWORD

Visit New Orleans at any time of the year – especially during Mardi Gras – and you will find yourself swept up in a swirl of excitement. This is not just the city that never sleeps; it is the city that never stands still. Jazz pours from open doorways, drifts from piano bars, seems to sizzle in the very air you breathe. And wherever there is music, there is food. Wonderful gutsy, glorious food. Rich in colour, often fiery but always full of flavour, Cajun cooking is unique.

Green pepper, celery and onions are favourite flavourings (used in combination so often that they are known as "The Holy Trinity"), but it is in spicing that the Cajun cook excels. Cayenne, black and white pepper and paprika are all grist to the cook's mill, and every family has its own spice mix.

With the Mississippi Delta on the doorstep, it comes as no surprise that seafood is a speciality. Redfish, catfish, crabs, snapper and sea bass come from the coastal waters, with the bayous providing freshwater fish and crayfish. Louisiana is famous for its oysters, which are particularly plump, sweet and succulent in the spring, when the beds are swept by the Mississippi flood waters.

When the early settlers made this area their home, they found plenty of game for the cooking pots. Smothered Rabbit, with its spicy onion and celery sauce, remains a popular dish, and small game birds such as quail are now farmed, along with poussin, duck and chicken. Louisianans are fond of pork, which was introduced by the early American settlers.

Cajuns love sweet, succulent vegetables; particularly corn, sweet potatoes and parsnips. Tomatoes, introduced by the Spanish, are also widely used, as is the okra that was contributed by West African slaves brought in to work the vast cotton plantations.

Sweet treats include Pecan Pie and the famous Pecan Nut Divinity Cake, both of which feature in this exciting collection of recipes.

This is more than a cookbook: it's an invitation, requesting your presence at a feast of fabulous flavours. Cajun cooking is one of the world's most exciting cuisines – enjoy it!

RUBY LE BOIS

INTRODUCTION

Like its sophisticated cousin, Creole cooking, Cajun cooking is predominantly French, with liberal dashes of Spanish, African and native American influences. But unlike Creole cooking, which originated in the fine kitchens of wealthy French cotton plantation owners and was honed in the restaurants they frequented, Cajun cooking came from peasant stock, from an intrepid and enterprising group of farmers and fishermen whose arrival in Louisiana was the result of adversity rather than adventure.

These were the Acadians, French men and women who settled in Acadia (later to become Nova Scotia) in 1620, only to find themselves ousted by the British in 1713. They fled south, many ending up in the "French triangle" of South-Western Louisiana, a place as hot and humid as Canada had been cold and bracing. The adaptable Acadians embraced their new home with enthusiasm, remodelling the recipes of their forefathers to include the local game and seafood. From native Americans they learned to gather wild herbs and berries, and how to use a mixture of ground sassafras and thyme (*filé*) as a thickener. West African cooks, brought to Louisiana to work the cotton plantations, introduced them to mysterious new vegetables, such as okra, which they called *n'gombo*. The name persists today as *gumbo*, a soup/stew made from seafood, meat, poultry or vegetables.

In the latter half of the 18th century, New Orleans was ruled by Spain, and new ingredients and cooking styles came on the scene. Acadians, now known as Cajuns, took this in their stride. They learned to love paella (a perfect dish for this part of the world, with its abundant rice and seafood), adapting it in their own inimitable fashion and giving it a new name, "Jambalaya", in recognition of the ham (*jambon*) which was almost always included.

While traditional French peasant dishes survived, Cajun cooks were scaling new heights. They had discovered peppers in all their rich and wondrous variety. Fresh chillies, sweet peppers, cayenne, paprika, ground black and white pepper – all were

investigated, then incorporated into a constantly evolving cuisine. They borrowed from Creole cooks, too, and the boundaries between the two culinary styles began to blur.

Today, while Cajun cooking continues to be more robust than its "citified" Creole counterpart, it, too, has its subtle side. Bisques, brochettes and featherlight beignets happily coexist

Two street scenes in New Orleans: the east Pontalba building in the French quarter (above) and early evening in bustling Bourbon Street (left).

with blackened fish and baked sweet potatoes. The roux, that famous French thickening and flavouring agent, is common to both cuisines. Oil, rather than the more conventional butter, is heated and stirred with flour in a black iron pan and the mixture allowed to darken, the depth of colour varying according to the individual recipe. Roux is so fundamental to both Cajun and Creole cooking that many cooks make up the various mixtures in bulk.

In 1803 New Orleans became part of the United States as a result of the Louisiana Purchase. With its cosmopolitan history, the city and its environs continued to attract immigrants from all over the globe. Each brought their cooking pots and favourite recipes, and each enriched – and was enriched by – Cajun cooking.

This marvellous trade continues today. Cajun cooks love experimenting with new ideas and ingredients, and expect all who try their recipes to do the same. So – if you find it difficult to obtain any of the ingredients in this book, do as those early Acadians did – adopt and adapt!

HOT PARSNIP FRITTERS ON BABY SPINACH

Fritters are a firm favourite of Cajun cooks, with their love for deep frying. The technique brings out the luscious sweetness of parsnips, here set on a walnut-dressed salad of tender baby spinach leaves.

INGREDIENTS
2 large parsnips
115g/4oz/1 cup plain flour
1 egg, separated
120ml/4fl oz/½ cup milk
115g/4oz baby spinach leaves
30ml/2 tbsp olive oil
15ml/1 tbsp walnut oil
15ml/1 tbsp sherry vinegar
oil for deep frying
15ml/1 tbsp coarsely chopped walnuts
salt, ground black pepper and
cayenne pepper

SERVES 4

1 Peel the parsnips, bring to the boil in a large pan of salted water and simmer for 10–15 minutes until tender but not mushy. Drain, cool and cut diagonally into slices about 5 x 1cm/2 x ½in.

2 Put the flour in a bowl, make a well in the centre and add the egg yolk. Mix in with a fork, gradually stirring in the surrounding flour. Begin adding the milk, while continuing to mix in the flour. Season with salt, and black and cayenne peppers, and then beat with a whisk until the batter is completely smooth.

3 Discard any baby spinach leaves that are discoloured or damaged, then wash the rest and dry them carefully. Place the leaves in a bowl. Make the dressing: in a screw-top jar, mix the olive and walnut oils, sherry vinegar, and salt and black pepper to taste. Shake the jar vigorously.

4 When ready to serve, whisk the egg white until it peaks softly. Fold in a little of the batter, then fold the white into the batter. Heat the oil for deep frying.

5 Toss the salad in the dressing. Arrange the dressed leaves on four salad plates and scatter with walnuts.

6 Dip the parsnip slices in the batter and fry a few at a time until puffy and golden. Drain on kitchen paper and keep warm. To serve, arrange the fritters on the salad.

SWEETCORN CAKES WITH GRILLED TOMATOES

I f you are short of time, use drained canned sweetcorn in place of the fresh corn on the cob in these delightful and tasty fritters.

INGREDIENTS
1 large corn on the cob
75g/3oz/⅔ cup plain flour
1 egg
a little milk
2 large, firm tomatoes
1 garlic clove
5ml/1 tsp dried oregano
30–45ml/2–3 tbsp oil, plus extra for
shallow frying
8 cupped iceberg lettuce leaves
salt and ground black pepper
shredded fresh basil leaves, to garnish

SERVES 4

1 Pull the husks and silk away from the corn, then hold the cob upright on a board and cut downwards with a heavy knife to strip off the kernels. Place in a pan of boiling water and cook for 3 minutes after the water has returned to the boil, then drain through a colander and rinse under cold running water to cool quickly.

2 Put the flour into a bowl, make a well in the centre and add the egg. Mix with a fork, gradually stirring in the flour, adding a little milk to make a soft dropping consistency. Add the sweetcorn and season.

3 Preheat the grill. Halve the tomatoes horizontally and make two or three criss-cross slashes across the cut side of each half. Crush the garlic and rub it, the oregano and some salt and pepper over the cut surface of each half, then trickle with oil and grill until lightly browned.

4 Meanwhile, heat some oil in a wide frying pan and drop a large spoonful of batter into the centre. Cook one cake at a time, over a low heat, turning as soon as the top is set. Drain on kitchen paper and keep warm while cooking the remaining cakes. The mixture should make at least eight sweetcorn cakes.

5 Put two lettuce leaves on each of four serving plates, place two sweetcorn cakes on top, garnish with basil and serve with a grilled tomato half.

CRAB BAYOU

Don't be tempted to use canned crab meat in this dish – the result will be disappointing. Fresh crab meat is now available in most supermarkets.

INGREDIENTS
450g/1lb fresh lump crab meat
3 hard-boiled egg yolks
5ml/1 tsp Dijon mustard
75g/3oz/6 tbsp butter or margarine, at room temperature
1.5ml/¼ tsp cayenne pepper
45ml/3 tbsp sherry
30ml/2 tbsp chopped fresh parsley
120ml/4fl oz/½ cup whipping cream
40g/1½oz/½ cup thinly sliced spring onions, including some of the green stems
50g/2oz/½ cup dried breadcrumbs
salt and ground black pepper

SERVES 6

1 Preheat the oven to 180°C/350°F/Gas 4. Pick over the crab meat and remove any shell or cartilage, keeping the pieces of crab as big as possible.

2 In a bowl, crumble the egg yolks with a fork. Add the mustard, 50g/2oz/4 tbsp of the butter or margarine, and the cayenne, and mash together to form a paste.

3 Mash in the sherry and parsley. Mix in the cream and spring onions. Stir in the crab meat. Season with salt and pepper.

4 Divide the mixture equally among six greased scallop shells or other individual baking dishes. Sprinkle with the dried breadcrumbs and dot with the remaining butter or margarine.

5 Bake for about 20 minutes until bubbling hot and golden brown.

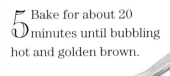

SWEETCORN AND CRAB BISQUE

A Louisiana classic, and certainly luxurious enough for a dinner party, which makes it well worth the trouble to prepare.

INGREDIENTS
4 large corn on the cob
2 bay leaves
1 cooked crab weighing about 1kg/2¼lb
25g/1oz/2 tbsp butter
15g/½oz/2 tbsp plain flour
300ml/½ pint/1¼ cups whipping cream
6 spring onions, shredded
salt, ground black and white pepper, and cayenne pepper
hot French bread, to serve (optional)

SERVES 8

1 Pull away the husks and silk from the corn, hold the cob upright on a board and cut downwards with a heavy knife to strip off the kernels, then set aside.

2 Put the stripped cobs into a deep saucepan with 2.5 litres/4¼ pints/10¼ cups cold water, the bay leaves and 10ml/2 tsp salt. Bring to the boil and leave to simmer until tender.

3 Pull away the two flaps between the big claws of the crab, stand it on its "nose" where the flaps were, and bang down firmly with the heel of your hand on the rounded end. Separate the crab from its top shell, keeping the shell.

4 Push out the mouth and abdominal sac immediately below the mouth, and discard. Pull away the gills around the central chamber and discard. Scrape out all the semi-liquid brown meat and keep it.

5 Crack the claws and extract all the white meat. Pick out the white meat from the central body. Set aside. Put the spidery legs and all the other pieces of shell into the pan with the corn cobs. Simmer for 15 minutes, then strain into a clean pan and boil rapidly to reduce to 2 litres/3⅓ pints/8 cups.

6 Meanwhile, melt the butter in a small pan, add the flour and stir constantly over a low heat until the roux is the colour of rich cream. Off the heat, stir in 250ml/8fl oz/1 cup of the stock. Return to the heat, stir until thickened, then stir into the pan of strained stock. Add the sweetcorn kernels, return to the boil and simmer for 5 minutes.

7 Add the crab meat, cream and spring onions and season with salt, black pepper and cayenne pepper. Return to the boil and simmer for 2 minutes. Serve immediately with hot French bread, if using.

"POPCORN" WITH BASIL MAYONNAISE

C rispy battered seafood is served with a rich, herby mayonnaise for dipping. This is an ideal dish for an informal supper party.

INGREDIENTS
900g/2lb raw crayfish tails, peeled, or
small prawns, peeled and deveined
2 eggs
250ml/8fl oz/1 cup dry white wine
50g/2oz/½ cup fine cornmeal
50g/2oz/½ cup plain flour
15ml/1 tbsp snipped fresh chives
1 garlic clove, minced
2.5ml/½ tsp fresh thyme leaves
1.5ml/¼ tsp salt
1.5ml/¼ tsp ground black pepper
1.5ml/¼ tsp cayenne pepper
oil for deep frying

FOR THE MAYONNAISE
1 egg yolk
10ml/2 tsp Dijon mustard
15ml/1 tbsp white wine vinegar
250ml/8fl oz/1 cup olive or vegetable oil
15g/½oz/½ cup basil leaves, chopped
salt and ground black pepper

SERVES 8

1 Rinse the crayfish tails or prawns in cold water. Drain well and set aside in a cool place until needed.

2 Using a fork, whisk together the eggs and dry white wine in a small bowl, then set aside in a cool place.

3 In a mixing bowl, combine the cornmeal, flour, chives, garlic, thyme, salt and pepper, and the cayenne pepper. Gradually whisk in the egg mixture, blending well. Cover the batter and then leave to stand for about 1 hour at room temperature.

4 For the mayonnaise, combine the egg yolk, mustard and vinegar in a mixing bowl. Add salt and pepper to taste. Add the oil in a thin stream, beating vigorously with a wire whisk. When the mixture is thick and smooth, stir in the basil. Cover and chill.

5 Heat 5–7.5cm/2–3in oil in a large frying pan or deep fryer to 190°C/375°F. Dip the seafood into the batter and fry in small batches for 2–3 minutes, turning to colour evenly until golden brown. Remove with a slotted spoon and drain on kitchen paper. Serve hot with the basil mayonnaise.

SWEETCORN AND PRAWN BISQUE

T his creamy soup is quite filling, so provide a light main course to follow if serving as a starter at a lunch or dinner party.

INGREDIENTS
30ml/2 tbsp olive oil
1 onion, chopped
50g/2oz/4 tbsp butter or margarine
25g/1oz/¼ cup plain flour
750ml/1¼ pints/3 cups fish or chicken
stock, or clam juice
250ml/8fl oz/1 cup milk
115g/4oz/1 cup peeled, cooked small
prawns, deveined if necessary
250g/9oz/1½ cups sweetcorn, fresh, frozen
or canned
2.5ml/½ tsp chopped fresh dill or thyme
120ml/4fl oz/½ cup single cream
salt and hot pepper sauce
fresh dill sprigs and prawns, to garnish

SERVES 4

1 Heat the olive oil in a large heavy-based saucepan. Add the onion and cook over a low heat for about 8–10 minutes until softened.

2 Meanwhile, melt the butter or margarine in a medium saucepan. Add the flour and stir with a wire whisk until blended. Cook for 1–2 minutes. Pour in the stock or clam juice, and milk and stir to blend. Bring to the boil over a medium heat and cook for 5–8 minutes, stirring frequently.

3 Cut each prawn in half and add to the onion with the sweetcorn and dill or thyme. Cook for 2–3 minutes, stirring occasionally. Remove the pan from the heat.

4 Add the sauce mixture to the prawn and sweetcorn mixture and stir to mix well. Remove 750ml/1¼ pints/3 cups of the soup and purée in a blender or food processor. Return it to the rest of the soup in the pan and stir well. Season with salt and hot pepper sauce to taste.

5 Add the cream and stir to blend. Heat the soup almost to boiling point, stirring frequently. Serve hot, garnished with sprigs of fresh dill and prawns.

GREEN HERB GUMBO

raditionally served at the end of Lent, this is a joyful, sweetly spiced and revitalizing dish.

INGREDIENTS
350g/12oz piece raw smoked gammon
30ml/2 tbsp cooking oil
1 large Spanish onion, roughly chopped
2–3 garlic cloves, crushed
5ml/1 tsp each dried oregano and thyme
2 bay leaves
2 cloves
2 celery sticks, finely sliced
1 green pepper, seeded and chopped
½ green cabbage, stalks removed and finely shredded
2 litres/3⅓ pints/8 cups light stock
200g/7oz spring greens or curly kale, finely shredded
200g/7oz Chinese mustard cabbage, finely shredded (see Cook's Tip)
200g/7oz spinach, shredded
1 bunch watercress, shredded
6 spring onions, finely shredded
25g/1oz/½ cup chopped fresh parsley
2.5ml/½ tsp ground allspice
5ml/1 tsp grated nutmeg
salt, ground black pepper and cayenne pepper
hot French bread or garlic bread, to serve

SERVES 6–8

1 Remove the fat and rind from the gammon in one piece and set aside. Dice the ham quite finely. Put the fat piece with the oil into a deep saucepan and heat until it sizzles. Stir in the diced ham, onion, garlic, oregano and thyme, and stir over a moderate heat for about 5 minutes.

2 Add the bay leaves, cloves, celery and green pepper and stir for about another 2–3 minutes, then add the cabbage and stock. Bring to the boil and simmer for 5 minutes.

3 Add the spring greens or curly kale and Chinese mustard cabbage, boil for a further 2 minutes, then add the spinach, watercress and spring onions. Lower the heat and simmer for 1 minute after it returns to the boil, then add the parsley, ground allspice and nutmeg, salt, black pepper and cayenne to taste.

4 Remove the piece of ham fat and, if you can find them, the cloves. Serve the gumbo immediately with hot French bread or garlic bread.

COOK'S TIP
Chinese mustard cabbage is available in some supermarkets, as well as from oriental shops and markets. If, however, you can't find it, substitute turnip tops or kohlrabi leaves.

FROMAJARDIS

These cheese-filled pastry parcels are ideal to serve at a drinks party. Try using a mixture of thyme, chives and sage in the filling.

INGREDIENTS
225g/8oz/2 cups plain flour
1.5ml/¼ tsp grated nutmeg
2.5ml/½ tsp salt
150g/5oz/10 tbsp cold butter
90–120ml/6–8 tbsp iced water

FOR THE FILLING
2 eggs
115g/4oz/1 cup grated Cheddar cheese
hot pepper sauce
15ml/1 tbsp chopped mixed fresh herbs

MAKES ABOUT 40

1 For the pastry, sift the flour, nutmeg and salt into a bowl. Using a pastry blender or two knives, cut the butter into the dry ingredients as quickly as possible until the mixture resembles coarse breadcrumbs.

2 Sprinkle 90ml/6 tbsp of the iced water over the flour mixture. Combine with a fork until the dough holds together. If the dough is too crumbly, add a little more water, 15ml/1 tbsp at a time. Gather the dough into a ball.

3 Divide the dough in half and pat each portion into a round. Wrap the rounds in greaseproof paper; chill for 20 minutes.

4 Preheat the oven to 220°C/425°F/Gas 7. For the filling, put the eggs in a bowl and beat well with a fork. Add the cheese, hot pepper sauce to taste, and the herbs.

5 On a lightly floured surface, roll out the dough to a thickness of 3mm/⅛in or less. Cut out rounds using a 7.5cm/3in pastry cutter or drinking glass.

6 Place 5ml/1 tsp of filling in the centre of each pastry round. Fold over to make half-moon shapes, and press the edges together with the prongs of a fork. A bit of filling may ooze through the seams.

7 Cut a few small slashes in the top of each pastry with the point of a sharp knife. Place on ungreased baking sheets. Bake for 18–20 minutes until the pastries start to darken slightly. To test, cut one in half; the pastry should be completely cooked through. Serve warm.

COOK'S TIP
The fromajardis may be made ahead of time. Leave them to cool on a wire rack and then store in an airtight container. Just before serving, reheat the pastries for 5–10 minutes in a preheated oven at 190°C/375°F/Gas 5.

FRIED FISH WITH TARTARE SAUCE AND HUSH PUPPIES

he story goes that fishermen would fry pieces of batter, then throw them to their dogs to hush them.

INGREDIENTS
115g/4oz/1 cup cornmeal
50g/2oz/½ cup plain flour
7.5ml/1½ tsp baking powder
1 garlic clove, crushed with 5ml/1 tsp salt
2 spring onions, finely shredded
1 egg, lightly beaten
about 75ml/5 tbsp milk
25g/1oz/2 tbsp butter

FOR THE FISH COATING
25g/1oz/¼ cup plain flour
25g/1oz/¼ cup cornflour
50g/2oz/½ cup cornmeal
2.5ml/½ tsp each dried oregano and thyme
5ml/1 tsp each salt, cayenne and paprika
10ml/2 tsp dry mustard powder
1 egg
120ml/4fl oz/½ cup milk

FOR THE FISH FILLETS
oil for deep frying
4 plaice fillets, skinned
lemon slices and flat leaf parsley,
to garnish
tartare sauce, to serve

SERVES 4

1 To make the hush puppy batter, mix together the cornmeal, flour and baking powder and stir in the crushed garlic and spring onions. Stir in the egg with a fork.

2 Heat 75ml/5 tbsp milk and the butter together slowly until the butter melts, then increase the heat and, when it boils, stir thoroughly into the dry ingredients, adding a little more milk if necessary to make a stiff dough. Leave to cool.

3 To make the fish coating, mix the flour, cornflour and cornmeal with the herbs and seasonings in a shallow dish. Beat the egg and milk together in another dish.

4 Scoop out pieces of hush puppy batter no bigger than a walnut and roll into balls between wetted hands. Heat the oil for deep frying. Fry the hush puppies in batches, until golden brown. They will swell in cooking, and it's important that they are cooked right to the middle, so don't have the oil fiercely hot to start with. It should sizzle and froth up round them as you drop them in, but not brown them at once. Drain on kitchen paper and keep warm.

5 Coat the fish fillets, first in the egg mixture and then in the flour and cornmeal coating mixture. Fry the fillets two at a time for 2–3 minutes on each side, until crisp and golden brown; drain on kitchen paper. Serve the fish fillets with the hush puppies and tartare sauce, garnished with lemon and parsley.

SPICED FISH

Cajun blackened fish is a speciality of Paul Prudhommes, a chef from New Orleans. Fillets of fish are coated with an aromatic blend of herbs and spices and pan-fried in butter.

INGREDIENTS
5ml/1 tsp dried thyme
5ml/1 tsp dried oregano
5ml/1 tsp ground black pepper
1.5ml/¼ tsp cayenne pepper
10ml/2 tsp paprika
2.5ml/½ tsp garlic salt
4 cod or red bream fillets, about 175g/
6oz each
75g/3oz/6 tbsp butter
½ red pepper, sliced
½ green pepper, sliced
fresh thyme, to garnish
grilled tomatoes and sweet potato purée,
to serve

SERVES 4

1 Place all the herbs, garlic salt and spices in a bowl and mix well. Dip the fish fillets in the spice mixture until lightly coated.

2 Heat 25g/1oz/2 tbsp of the butter in a large frying pan, add the peppers and fry for 4–5 minutes until softened. Remove the peppers and keep warm.

3 Add the remaining butter to the pan and heat until sizzling. Add the fish fillets and fry over a moderate heat for 3–4 minutes on each side, until browned and cooked.

4 Transfer the fish fillets to a warmed serving dish, surround with the fried red and green pepper slices and garnish with fresh thyme. Serve the spiced fish with some grilled tomato halves and creamy sweet potato purée.

COOK'S TIP
This blend of herbs and spices can be used to flavour any fish steaks or fillets and could also be used to jazz up pan-fried prawns.

FISH STEAKS WITH DILL-MUSTARD SAUCE

C atfish is the favourite choice of a firm white fish in Cajun cooking. Cod is a good alternative. Here, fish is fried to a light golden crust in butter and served with a pungent mustard sauce.

INGREDIENTS
30ml/2 tbsp milk
4 catfish or cod steaks, about
175g/6oz each
25g/1oz/2 tbsp plain flour
10ml/2 tsp mustard powder
50g/2oz/4 tbsp butter
salt and ground black pepper
lemon wedges and fresh dill sprigs,
to garnish

FOR THE SAUCE
30ml/2 tbsp Dijon mustard
150ml/¼ pint/⅔ cup mayonnaise
30ml/2 tbsp finely chopped fresh dill

SERVES 4

1 Mix all the ingredients for the sauce in a small bowl and put to one side until required.

2 Put the milk in a soup plate and lay the fish steaks in it. On a separate plate, mix the flour, mustard powder and seasoning.

3 Melt the butter in a frying pan. Turn the fish in the milk and dip immediately in the flour mixture; shake off any excess.

4 When the butter sizzles, fry the fish steaks for 2–3 minutes on each side until the outside is crisp and pale golden and you can just pull the flesh from the bone with the sharp tip of a knife. Work in two batches if you need to, keeping the fish warm until ready to serve.

5 Serve as soon as possible, garnished with lemon wedges and sprigs of dill. Hand the sauce round separately.

CRAYFISH OR PRAWN ETOUFFÉE

touffer means "to smother", and this seafood dish is certainly smothered in delectable flavours.

INGREDIENTS
1.2kg/2½lb raw crayfish or prawns in the shell, with heads left on
75ml/3fl oz/⅓ cup vegetable oil
40g/1½oz/⅓ cup flour
175g/6oz/¾ cup chopped onions
50g/2oz/¼ cup chopped green pepper
50g/2oz/¼ cup chopped celery
1 garlic clove, crushed
120ml/4fl oz/½ cup dry white wine
25g/1oz/2 tbsp butter or margarine
25g/1oz/½ cup chopped fresh parsley
15g/½oz/¼ cup snipped fresh chives
salt and hot pepper sauce
crayfish and flat leaf parsley, to garnish
rice, to serve

SERVES 6

1 Peel and devein the crayfish or prawns; reserve the heads and shells. Place the seafood in a bowl, cover and chill.

2 Put the heads and shells in a large pan with 750ml/1¼ pints/3 cups water. Bring to the boil, cover and simmer for 15 minutes. Strain and reserve 350ml/12fl oz/1½ cups of the stock.

3 To make the Cajun roux, heat the oil in a heavy cast-iron frying pan or steel saucepan. (Do not use a non-stick pan.)

4 When hot, gradually add the flour, and blend to a smooth paste using a long-handled flat-ended wooden spoon.

5 Cook over a moderately low heat for about 25–40 minutes, stirring constantly, until the roux reaches the desired colour. It will gradually deepen in colour from light beige to tan, to a deeper, redder brown. When it reaches the colour of peanut butter, remove the pan from the heat and immediately mix in the onions, pepper and celery. Continue stirring to prevent further darkening.

6 Return the pan to a low heat. Add the garlic and cook for 1–2 minutes, stirring constantly. Add the seafood stock and blend well with a wire whisk. Then whisk in the dry white wine.

7 Bring to the boil, stirring, and simmer for about 3–4 minutes until the sauce is thickened. Remove from the heat.

8 In a large heavy-based saucepan, melt the butter or margarine. Add the crayfish or prawns, stir, and cook for about 2–3 minutes. Stir in the parsley and chives.

9 Add the sauce and stir well. Season with salt and hot pepper sauce to taste. Simmer for 3–4 minutes. Serve hot on a bed of rice, garnished with crayfish and parsley.

TROUT WITH PECAN NUT BUTTER

This is the Cajun version of the classic French dish of trout with almonds and produces a subtly spiced and herby supper dish.

INGREDIENTS
FOR THE PECAN NUT BUTTER
50g/2oz/½ cup shelled pecan nut halves, roasted
50g/2oz/4 tbsp unsalted butter
10ml/2 tsp Worcestershire sauce
5ml/1 tsp lemon juice

FOR THE TROUT FILLETS
4 large trout fillets, about 175g/6oz each
10ml/2 tsp paprika
5ml/1 tsp cayenne pepper
5ml/1 tsp dried oregano
pinch of dried thyme
2.5ml/½ tsp garlic salt
5ml/1 tsp salt
ground black pepper
1 egg
120ml/4fl oz/½ cup milk
40g/1½oz/3 tbsp plain flour
oil for shallow frying

SERVES 4

1 Finely chop the pecan nuts in a blender or food processor. Add the butter, Worcestershire sauce and lemon juice, and blend well. Scrape out on to clear film, roll into a sausage, wrap and chill.

2 Rinse the trout fillets under cold running water, then pat dry. Mix the paprika, cayenne, oregano, thyme and garlic salt with the salt and ground black pepper. Sprinkle a pinch over each fillet.

3 Beat the egg and milk in a shallow dish; add 5ml/1 tsp of the spice mix. In another dish, combine the remaining spice mix with the flour.

4 Heat the oil for shallow frying in a frying pan. Dip the trout fillets in the egg mixture, then in the seasoned flour, shaking off any excess. Fry, then drain on kitchen paper and keep warm. Serve the fillets with a slice of pecan butter on each.

OYSTER AND BACON BROCHETTES

S ix oysters per person makes a good starter, served with the seasoned oyster liquor to trickle over the skewers. Serve nine oysters per person with a cool salad as a main course.

INGREDIENTS
36 live oysters
18 thin-cut rashers rindless streaky bacon
115g/4oz/1 cup plain flour
15ml/1 tbsp paprika
5ml/1 tsp cayenne pepper
5ml/1 tsp salt
5ml/1 tsp garlic salt
10ml/2 tsp dried oregano
ground black pepper
oil for shallow frying
celery leaves and red chillies, to garnish

FOR THE SAUCE
½ red chilli, seeded and very finely chopped
2 spring onions, very finely chopped
30ml/2 tbsp finely chopped fresh parsley
juice of ¼–½ lemon
salt and ground black pepper

SERVES 4–6

1 Shuck the oysters over a bowl. Wrap your hand in a dish towel and cup the deep shell of each oyster in it. Twist the point of a strong short-bladed knife into the hinge between the shells. Push the knife in and cut the muscle, holding the shell closed. Tip the liquor from the deep shell into the bowl. Cut the flesh free from the shell. Discard the shells.

2 For the sauce, mix the chilli, spring onions and parsley into the oyster liquor and sharpen with lemon juice. Season and transfer to a small bowl.

3 Halve the bacon rashers widthways, wrap round each oyster, then thread on to four or six skewers. On a plate, mix the flour with the paprika, cayenne pepper, salt, garlic salt, oregano and black pepper. Roll the skewers in it, shaking off the excess.

4 Heat 2.5cm/1in depth of oil in a wide frying pan and fry the skewers in small batches for about 3–4 minutes over a moderately high heat, turning until crisp and brown. Drain on kitchen paper and serve garnished with the celery leaves and red chillies and accompanied by the sauce.

PRAWN-STUFFED AUBERGINE

The rich, creamy texture of aubergines is beautifully offset by a herby and slightly spicy prawn filling in this impressive looking and great-tasting dish.

INGREDIENTS

2 large firm aubergines, of equal size
30ml/2 tbsp lemon juice
40g/1½oz/3 tbsp butter or margarine
225g/8oz raw prawns, peeled and deveined
40g/1½oz/½ cup thinly sliced spring onions, including some green stems
4 tomatoes, chopped
1 garlic clove, crushed
10g/¼oz/¼ cup chopped fresh parsley
10g/¼oz/¼ cup chopped fresh basil
pinch of grated nutmeg
hot pepper sauce
50g/2oz/½ cup dried breadcrumbs
rice, to serve
salt and ground black pepper

SERVES 4

1 Preheat the oven to 190°C/375°F/Gas 5. Cut the aubergines in half lengthways. With a small sharp knife, cut around the inside edge of each aubergine half, about 1cm/½in from the skin. Carefully scoop out the flesh, leaving a shell 1cm/½in thick.

2 Immerse the aubergine shells, skin-side up, in cold water to prevent them from becoming discoloured.

3 Chop the scooped-out aubergine flesh coarsely, toss with the lemon juice and set aside until needed.

4 Melt 25g/1oz/2 tbsp of the butter or margarine in a frying pan. Add the prawns and sauté until pink, for about 2–3 minutes, turning so they cook evenly. Remove the prawns with a slotted spoon and set aside.

5 Add the spring onions to the frying pan and cook over a medium heat for 2 minutes, stirring constantly. Add the tomatoes, garlic and parsley and cook for a further 5 minutes.

6 Add the chopped aubergine, basil and nutmeg. If necessary, add a little water to prevent the vegetables from sticking. Mix well. Cover and simmer for 8–10 minutes, then remove from the heat.

7 Cut each prawn into two. Stir into the vegetable mixture. Season with salt, black pepper and hot pepper sauce.

8 Lightly oil a shallow baking dish large enough to hold the aubergine halves in one layer. Drain and dry the aubergine shells and arrange in the dish.

9 Make a layer of breadcrumbs in each shell. Add a layer of the prawn mixture. Repeat, and finish with a layer of crumbs.

10 Dot with the remaining butter or margarine. Bake for about 20–25 minutes until bubbling hot and golden brown on top. Serve accompanied by rice.

FRIED FISH WITH PIQUANT SAUCE

F ried until golden brown, firm-textured fish fillets are here accompanied by a cold, sharp-tasting sauce.

INGREDIENTS
FOR THE FRIED FISH
1 egg
50ml/2fl oz/¼ cup olive oil
squeeze of lemon juice
2.5ml/½ tsp chopped fresh dill or parsley
4 catfish or cod fillets, about 175g/6oz each
50g/2oz/½ cup flour
25g/1oz/2 tbsp butter or margarine
salt and ground black pepper

FOR THE SAUCE
1 egg yolk
30ml/2 tbsp Dijon mustard
30ml/2 tbsp white wine vinegar
10ml/2 tsp paprika
120ml/4fl oz/½ cup olive or vegetable oil
30ml/2 tbsp creamed horseradish
2.5ml/½ tsp crushed garlic
50g/2oz/¼ cup chopped celery
30ml/2 tbsp tomato ketchup
2.5ml/½ tsp ground black pepper
2.5ml/½ tsp salt
mixed salad, to serve

SERVES 4

1 For the sauce, combine the egg yolk, mustard, vinegar and paprika in a mixing bowl. Add the oil in a thin stream, beating vigorously with a wire whisk to blend it in.

2 When the mixture is smooth and thick, beat in all the other sauce ingredients. Cover and chill until ready to serve.

3 Combine the egg, 15ml/1 tbsp of the olive oil, the lemon juice, herbs and a little salt and pepper in a shallow dish. Beat until well combined.

4 Dip both sides of each fish fillet in the egg and herb mixture, then coat lightly with flour, shaking off the excess.

5 Heat the butter or margarine with the remaining olive oil in a large heavy-based frying pan. Add the fillets and fry for about 8–10 minutes until golden brown and cooked on both sides.

6 Transfer the fish to warmed serving plates and spoon some sauce over the top of each. Serve with a mixed salad.

SEAFOOD AND SAUSAGE GUMBO

T his is a classic Cajun gumbo, with mussels, prawns, crab meat and chunks of wonderfully spicy sausage – a memorable dish.

INGREDIENTS

450g/1lb live mussels
450g/1lb prawns
1 cooked crab weighing about 1kg/2¼lb
salt
1 small bunch parsley, leaves chopped
and stalks reserved
150ml/¼ pint/⅔ cup oil
115g/4oz/1 cup plain flour
1 green pepper, seeded and chopped
1 large onion, chopped
2 celery sticks, chopped
3 garlic cloves, finely chopped
75g/3oz smoked spiced sausage, skinned
and sliced
6 spring onions, finely chopped
cayenne pepper
Tabasco sauce
salt
cooked rice, to serve
parsley, to garnish

SERVES 10–12

1 Wash the mussels in several changes of cold water, scrubbing away any barnacles and pulling off the black "beards" that protrude between the shells. Discard any broken mussels or any that are not closed.

2 Heat 250ml/8fl oz/1 cup water in a pan. When it boils, add the mussels, cover tightly and cook for about 3 minutes over high heat, shaking often. As the mussels open, lift them out with tongs into a sieve set over a bowl. Discard any mussels that have not opened.

3 Shell the mussels, discarding the shells. Return the liquid from the bowl to the pan and make the quantity up to 2 litres/3½ pints/9 cups with water.

4 Shell the prawns and put the shells and heads into the pan. Remove the meat from the crab, separating the brown and white meat. Add the crab shell to the pan with 10ml/2 tsp salt. Bring to the boil, add the parsley stalks and simmer for 15 minutes. Cool, then strain. Make the liquid up to 2 litres/3½ pints/9 cups water.

5 Make a roux with the oil and flour and stir until golden. Add the pepper, onion, celery and garlic and cook for 3 minutes. Add the sausage. Reheat the stock.

6 Add the brown crabmeat to the roux with the stock. Simmer for 30 minutes, then add the seafood, onions and seasoning. Serve with rice and garnish with parsley.

GLAZED DUCK BREASTS

Sweet potatoes accompany succulent sliced duck breast in this delicious dish. Choose a long, cylindrically shaped tuber.

INGREDIENTS

2 duck breast fillets, about 175g/6oz each
1 pink-skinned sweet potato, about
400g/14oz
30ml/2 tbsp redcurrant jelly
5ml/1 tsp hot chilli sauce
15ml/1 tbsp sherry vinegar
50g/2oz/4 tbsp butter, melted
coarse sea salt and ground black pepper
green salad, to serve

SERVES 2

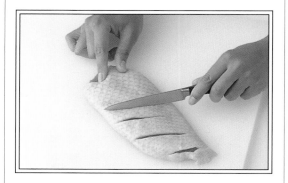

1 Slash the duck breast skin diagonally at 2.5cm/1in intervals and rub salt and pepper into the skin and cuts. Preheat the grill with the shelf placed so that the meat will be 7.5–10cm/3–4in from the heat.

2 Scrub the sweet potato and cut into 1cm/½in thick slices, discarding the rounded ends.

3 Grill the meat, skin-side up first, for 5 minutes, then flesh-side up for 8–10 minutes, according to how pink you like your duck.

4 Meanwhile for the glaze, warm the redcurrant jelly, hot chilli sauce and sherry vinegar together in a heatproof bowl set in a pan of hot water, stirring to mix them as the jelly melts.

5 Remove the grill pan from the heat, turn the duck breasts skin-side up and paint with the glaze. Return to the grill and cook for a further 2–3 minutes until the glaze caramelizes. Transfer the duck breasts to a serving plate and keep warm.

6 Brush the sweet potato slices with melted butter and arrange in the grill pan. Sprinkle with coarse sea salt and place one level higher under the grill than the duck breasts were.

7 Cook the sweet potatoes for 4–5 minutes on each side until soft, brushing with more butter and sprinkling with sea salt and black pepper when you turn them.

8 Slice the glazed duck breast fillets and serve them with the grilled sweet potatoes and a fresh green salad on the side.

SMOTHERED RABBIT

Game has always formed a big part of the Cajun diet – it was the only meat available to the early settlers. The smothering technique gives plenty of flavour to a domestic rabbit.

INGREDIENTS
10ml/2 tsp salt
2.5ml/½ tsp garlic salt
2.5ml/½ tsp dried oregano
good pinch each of ground black pepper
and cayenne pepper
1 rabbit, skinned, cleaned and cut into
8 pieces
50g/2oz/½ cup plain flour
60ml/4 tbsp oil
1 onion, chopped
1 celery stick, chopped
1 large garlic clove, crushed
1 bay leaf
350ml/12fl oz/1½ cups chicken stock
3 spring onions, shredded
30ml/2 tbsp chopped fresh parsley
mange-touts and crusty bread, to serve

SERVES 4

1 Mix the salt, garlic salt, oregano, black pepper and cayenne together. Sprinkle the rabbit pieces lightly, using about half the seasoning mix, and pat it in thoroughly with your fingers.

2 Put the rest of the seasoning mix with the flour into a plastic bag, shake to mix, then shake the pieces of rabbit in this to dredge them, shaking off and reserving the excess until needed.

3 Heat the oil in a heavy flameproof casserole and fry the rabbit pieces, in batches, until browned on all sides. Set aside on a plate.

4 When all the rabbit is browned, cook the chopped onion and celery in the same pan for 5 minutes, stirring often. Add the garlic and bay leaf.

5 Heat the stock. Add 15ml/1 tbsp of the seasoned flour to the oil in the pan and stir over the heat for 1 minute. Off the heat, gradually stir in some of the stock. When the sauce loosens, return to the heat and add the remaining stock, stirring constantly until boiling point is reached.

6 Lower the heat, return the rabbit pieces to the casserole, cover and simmer for about 1 hour, until the rabbit is very tender.

7 Check the seasoning and stir in the spring onions and parsley. Serve with the mange-touts and crusty bread.

CHICKEN SAUCE PIQUANTE

S auce Piquante goes with everything that runs, flies or swims in Louisiana – you will even find Alligator Sauce Piquante on menus. It is based on the brown Cajun roux and has red chillies to give it heat; vary the heat by the number you use.

INGREDIENTS
4 chicken legs or 2 legs and 2 breasts
75ml/5 tbsp oil
50g/2oz/½ cup plain flour
1 onion, chopped
2 celery sticks, sliced
1 green pepper, seeded and diced
2 garlic cloves, crushed
1 bay leaf
2.5ml/½ tsp dried thyme
2.5ml/½ tsp dried oregano
1–2 red chillies, seeded and finely chopped
400g/14oz can tomatoes, chopped, with their juice
300ml/½ pint/1¼ cups chicken stock
salt and ground black pepper
watercress, to garnish
boiled potatoes, to serve

SERVES 4

1 Halve the chicken legs through the joint, or the breasts across the middle, to give eight pieces.

2 In a heavy frying pan, fry the chicken pieces in the oil until brown on all sides, lifting them out and setting them aside as they are done.

3 Strain the oil from the pan into a heavy flameproof casserole. Heat it and stir in the flour. Stir constantly over low heat until the roux is the colour of peanut butter.

4 When the roux reaches the right stage, add the onion, celery and green pepper and cook, stirring, for 2–3 minutes.

5 Add the garlic, bay leaf, thyme, oregano and chilli(es). Stir for 1 minute, then add the tomatoes with their juice.

6 Gradually stir in the stock. Add the chicken pieces, cover and leave to simmer for 45 minutes, until the chicken is tender. If there is too much sauce or it is too runny, remove the lid for the last 10–15 minutes of the cooking time and increase the heat a little to concentrate the sauce.

7 Check the seasoning and serve garnished with watercress and accompanied by boiled potatoes.

POUSSINS WITH DIRTY RICE

This rice is called dirty not because of the bits in it but because jazz is called "dirty music", and the rice here is certainly jazzed up.

INGREDIENTS
FOR THE RICE
60ml/4 tbsp cooking oil
25g/1oz/¼ cup plain flour
50g/2oz/4 tbsp butter
1 large onion, chopped
2 celery sticks, chopped
1 green pepper, seeded and diced
2 garlic cloves, crushed
200g/7oz minced pork
225g/8oz chicken livers, sliced
salt, ground black pepper and
Tabasco sauce
300ml/½ pint/1¼ cups chicken stock
4 spring onions, shredded
45ml/3 tbsp chopped fresh parsley
225g/8oz/generous 1 cup American long
grain rice, cooked

FOR THE BIRDS
4 poussins
2 bay leaves, halved
25g/1oz/2 tbsp butter
1 lemon
salt and ground black pepper

SERVES 4

1 In a small heavy saucepan, make a roux with 30ml/2 tbsp of the oil and the flour. When it is a chestnut-brown colour, remove the pan from the heat and place it at once on a cold surface.

2 Heat the remaining oil with the butter in a frying pan and stir-fry the onion, celery and green pepper for about 5 minutes.

3 Add the garlic and pork and stir-fry for 5 minutes, breaking up the pork and stirring to cook it all over.

4 Add the livers and fry for 2–3 minutes until they have changed colour. Season with salt, pepper and Tabasco sauce.

5 Stir the roux into the pan; gradually add the stock. When it bubbles, cover and cook for 30 minutes; stir occasionally. Then uncover the pan and cook for a further 15 minutes, stirring frequently.

6 Preheat the oven to 200°C/400°F/Gas 6. Mix the spring onions and parsley into the meat mixture and stir it all into the cooked rice, mixing well.

7 Put ½ bay leaf and 15ml/1 tbsp rice into each poussin. Rub the outside with the butter and season with salt and pepper.

8 Put the birds on a rack in a roasting tin, squeeze the juice from the lemon over them and roast for 35–40 minutes, basting twice with the pan juices.

9 Put the remaining rice into a shallow ovenproof dish, cover, and place on a low shelf in the oven for about the last 15–20 minutes of the birds' cooking time.

10 Serve the birds on a bed of dirty rice with the roasting pan juices (drained of fat) poured over.

BLACKENED CHICKEN BREASTS

T he chicken breast pieces are fried quite quickly in this dish, causing the outside to become black and crispy while the inside remains soft and deliciously juicy.

INGREDIENTS

6 skinless, boneless chicken breast halves
75g/3oz/6 tbsp butter or margarine
5ml/1 tsp garlic powder
10ml/2 tsp onion powder
5ml/1 tsp cayenne pepper
10ml/2 tsp paprika
7.5ml/1½ tsp salt
2.5ml/½ tsp white pepper
5ml/1 tsp black pepper
1.5ml/¼ tsp ground cumin
5ml/1 tsp dried thyme
salad, to serve

SERVES 6

1 Slice each chicken breast piece in half horizontally, making two pieces of about the same thickness. Flatten slightly with the heel of your hand.

2 Melt the butter or margarine in a small saucepan, being very careful that it does not burn.

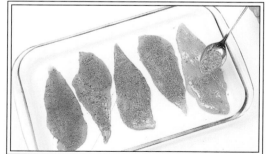

3 Combine all the remaining ingredients in a bowl. Brush the chicken pieces on both sides with melted butter or margarine, then sprinkle with the seasoning mixture.

4 Heat a large heavy frying pan over a high heat, with no fat in it, until a drop of water sprinkled on the surface sizzles. This will take 5–8 minutes.

5 Drizzle a teaspoon of melted butter on each chicken piece. Place them in the frying pan in an even layer, two or three at a time. Cook for about 2–3 minutes until the underside begins to blacken. Turn and cook the other side for a further 2–3 minutes. Keep the cooked pieces hot while cooking the remaining pieces. Serve hot with salad.

CHICKEN JAMBALAYA

T he secret of a good jambalaya lies in ensuring that the rice grains are well coated in oil before adding the liquid. This way they won't stick together while cooking.

INGREDIENTS

1.2kg/2½lb fresh chicken
1½ onions
1 bay leaf
1 parsley sprig
4 black peppercorns
30ml/2 tbsp vegetable oil
2 garlic cloves, chopped
1 green pepper, seeded and chopped
1 celery stick, chopped
225g/8oz/generous 1 cup long grain rice
115g/4oz chorizo sausage, sliced
115g/4oz/⅔ cup chopped, cooked ham
400g/14oz can chopped tomatoes with herbs
2.5ml/½ tsp hot chilli powder
2.5ml/½ tsp cumin seeds
2.5ml/½ tsp ground cumin
5ml/1 tsp dried thyme
115g/4oz/1 cup cooked, peeled prawns
dash of Tabasco sauce
chopped parsley, to garnish
salt and ground black pepper

SERVES 4

1 Place the chicken in a large flameproof casserole; pour in 600ml/1 pint/2½ cups water. Add ½ onion, bay leaf, parsley and peppercorns and bring to the boil. Cover and simmer for about 1½ hours.

2 When the chicken is cooked, lift it out of the stock, skin, bone and chop the meat. Strain the stock, cool and reserve.

3 Chop the remaining onion and heat the oil in a large frying pan. Add the onion, garlic, green pepper and celery. Fry for about 5 minutes, then stir in the rice. Add the sausage, ham and chopped chicken and fry for a further 2–3 minutes, stirring frequently.

4 Add the tomatoes and 300ml/½ pint/ 1¼ cups of the stock and add the chilli, cumin and thyme. Bring to the boil, cover and simmer for 20 minutes, or until the rice is tender and the liquid absorbed.

5 Stir in the prawns and Tabasco. Cook for 5 minutes, then season and serve.

LOUISIANA RICE

Some of the minced pork becomes slightly crispy in this rice dish, providing a variety of textures in a one-pan meal.

INGREDIENTS

60ml/4 tbsp vegetable oil
1 small aubergine, diced
225g/8oz minced pork
115g/4oz chicken thigh, chopped
1 red pepper, seeded and chopped
2 sticks celery, chopped
1 onion, chopped
1 garlic clove, crushed
5ml/1 tsp cayenne pepper
5ml/1 tsp paprika
5ml/1 tsp black pepper
2.5ml/½ tsp salt
5ml/1 tsp dried thyme
2.5ml/½ tsp dried oregano
475ml/16fl oz/2 cups chicken stock
225g/8oz chicken livers, chopped
150g/5oz/scant ¾ cup long grain rice
1 bay leaf
45ml/3 tbsp chopped fresh parsley
bay leaves, to garnish

SERVES 4

1 Heat the oil in a frying pan until very hot, then add the aubergine and stir-fry for about 5 minutes.

2 Add the pork and cook for 6–8 minutes, until browned. Add the chicken, mix well, cover, and cook for 10 minutes.

3 Add the pepper, celery, onion, garlic and all the spices and herbs. Cover and cook over a high heat for 5–6 minutes, stirring frequently from the base of the pan.

4 Stir in the stock, cover and cook for 6 minutes. Add the livers; cook for about 2 minutes. Add the rice and bay leaf.

5 Cover and simmer for 6 minutes. Turn off the heat and leave for another 15 minutes. Remove the bay leaf and stir in the parsley. Garnish with bay leaves. Serve hot.

PORK CHOPS WITH LEMON AND GARLIC SAUCE

This great recipe comes from the McIlhenny family, producers of Tabasco sauce. They like their food hot: cautious cooks can start off with less Tabasco, adding more at the end of cooking.

INGREDIENTS

4 pork chops, about 175g/6oz each
115g/4oz/½ cup butter
½ lemon
15ml/1 tbsp Worcestershire sauce
7.5ml/1½ tsp Tabasco sauce
1 garlic clove, finely chopped
salt and ground black pepper
grilled peppers and tomatoes, to serve

SERVES 4

1 Preheat the grill. Arrange the chops in the grill pan but do not place them under the grill.

2 Melt the butter in a small non-aluminium saucepan. Squeeze in the juice of the lemon and bring to simmering point.

3 Add the sauces and the garlic and, without browning the garlic, continue cooking over low heat for 5 minutes. Season.

4 Brush the tops of the chops liberally with the sauce, place the pan under the grill and cook for about 5 minutes until they begin to brown.

5 Turn the chops and brush with more sauce. Grill for a further 5 minutes or so, depending on the thickness of the chops. You can trickle a little more of the sauce over to serve. Serve the chops with grilled peppers and tomatoes.

ROAST PORK WITH CAJUN STUFFING

T he familiar trinity of onion, celery and green pepper gives a Cajun flavour to this handsome roast – complete with crackling.

INGREDIENTS
1.5kg/3–3½lb boned loin of pork
15ml/1 tbsp salt
5ml/1 tsp each ground black pepper,
cayenne pepper, paprika and
dried oregano
30ml/2 tbsp cooking oil or
25g/1oz/2 tbsp lard
1 small onion, finely chopped
1 celery stick, finely chopped
½ green pepper, seeded and
finely chopped
1 garlic clove, crushed

SERVES 6

1 If the pork is already tied up, untie it. Score the pork skin closely to make good crackling (you can ask your butcher to do this). Rub 10ml/2 tsp of the salt into the skin the night before if you can or, if not, as far in advance of cooking as possible on the day. If the meat has been chilled overnight, stand it in an airy place at room temperature for at least 2 hours before cooking.

2 Preheat the oven to 220°C/425°F/Gas 7. Mix the black pepper, cayenne, paprika and oregano with the remaining salt and rub over the meaty side of the meat.

3 Heat the oil or lard and gently fry the onion, celery and green pepper for about 5 minutes, adding the garlic for the last minute of cooking time.

4 Spread the softened vegetable mixture evenly over the inside of the meat, right up to the edges.

5 Carefully roll up the loin of pork, skin-side out, and tie in several places so that it holds its shape while cooking.

6 Roast the meat on a rack in a roasting tin. After 30 minutes, reduce the oven temperature to 180°C/350°F/Gas 4. Baste with the pan juices after 15 minutes and again every 20 minutes.

7 The overall roasting time will be about 2 hours. If the crackling does not go crisp and bubbly in the latter stages, increase the oven temperature a little for the last 20–30 minutes.

8 Allow the meat to rest in a warm place for 10–15 minutes before carving. This sets the juices.

MAQUE CHOUX

A Cajun classic, good with ham and chicken. Some cooks add a little sugar to heighten the sweetness, but for most, the natural sweetness of the sweetcorn is enough.

INGREDIENTS

50g/2oz/4 tbsp butter
1 large onion, finely chopped
1 green pepper, seeded and diced
2 large tomatoes, skinned and chopped
450g/1lb/4 cups frozen sweetcorn
kernels, thawed
120ml/4fl oz/½ cup milk
salt, ground black pepper and
cayenne pepper

SERVES 4–6

1 Melt half the butter in a large pan and soften the onion in it, stirring regularly over a low heat for about 10 minutes until it begins to turn pale gold. Add the green pepper and stir over the heat for a further minute, then add the tomatoes and leave to cook gently while preparing the sweetcorn.

2 Put the sweetcorn kernels and milk into a blender or food processor and process in brief bursts to break up the kernels to a porridgy consistency.

3 Stir the sweetcorn mixture thoroughly into the pan and cook, partly covered, over a low heat for 20 minutes. Stir regularly, making sure that it does not stick to the base of the pan. If the mixture becomes too dry, add a little more milk. If it is rather wet in the latter stages, uncover, increase the heat a little and stir constantly for the last 5 minutes to thicken it.

4 Stir in the rest of the butter and season generously with salt, black pepper and cayenne. Serve hot.

BAKED SWEET POTATOES

S weet potatoes go well with all of the favourite Cajun seasonings: plenty of salt, white pepper as well as black and cayenne pepper, and lavish quantities of butter. Serve each person with half a potato as an accompaniment to meat, sausages or fish, or a whole one as a supper dish, perhaps topped with crispy bacon.

INGREDIENTS
3 sweet potatoes, about 450g/1lb each
75g/3oz/6 tbsp butter, sliced
salt and black, white and
cayenne peppers
flat leaf parsley, to garnish

SERVES 3–6

1 Wash the potatoes, leaving them wet. Rub salt into the skins and prick them all over. Place on the middle oven shelf. Turn on the oven at 200°C/400°F/Gas 6 and bake for 1 hour, until the flesh feels soft.

2 The potatoes can either be served in halves or whole. For halves, split each one lengthways and make close diagonal cuts in the flesh of each half. Then spread with slices of butter, and work the butter and seasonings roughly into the cuts.

3 Alternatively, if the potatoes are to be served whole, make an incision along the length of each potato. Open them slightly and put in butter slices along the length, seasoning with salt and black, white and cayenne pepper. Garnish with parsley.

ROASTED POTATOES, PEPPERS AND SHALLOTS

Based on a dish which is served at the Commander's Palace, this is in the new, rather more elegant style of New Orleans restaurant cooking.

INGREDIENTS

500g/1¼lb waxy potatoes
12 shallots
2 yellow peppers
corn oil or olive oil
2 sprigs fresh rosemary
salt and ground black pepper

SERVES 4

COOK'S TIP
Although lamb does not feature prominently in Cajun cooking, this would certainly be a fine all-in-one vegetable dish to accompany it. It would also be good with roast chicken.

1 Preheat the oven to 200°C/400°F/Gas 6. Wash the potatoes and then blanch for 5 minutes in boiling water. Drain and, when they are cool enough to handle, skin and halve them lengthways.

2 Peel the shallots, allowing them to fall into their natural segments. Cut each yellow pepper lengthways into eight strips, discarding the seeds and pith.

3 Oil a shallow ovenproof dish thoroughly with corn or olive oil (corn oil is more authentic, olive oil tastes better). Assemble the potatoes and peppers in alternating rows and stud with the shallots.

4 Cut the rosemary sprigs into 5cm/2in lengths and tuck among the vegetables. Season the dish generously with corn or olive oil, salt and pepper, and bake in the oven, uncovered, for 30–40 minutes until all the vegetables are tender.

SPOONBREAD

This tasty cornmeal bread is so delightfully light that it has to be served with a spoon. Make sure you provide generous quantities of good quality butter to go with it.

INGREDIENTS
600ml/1 pint/2½ cups milk
130g/3½oz/1 cup yellow cornmeal
75g/3oz/6 tbsp butter or margarine
5ml/1 tsp salt
7.5ml/1½ tsp baking powder
3 eggs, separated
butter, to serve

SERVES 4

1 Preheat the oven to 190°C/375°F/Gas 5. Heat the milk in a heavy-based saucepan. Just before it boils, beat in the cornmeal with a wire whisk. Cook over a low heat for about 10 minutes, stirring constantly.

2 Remove the pan from the heat and then beat in the butter or margarine, the salt and the baking powder, whisking well until the mixture is completely smooth and the butter or margarine has melted.

3 Add the egg yolks, one at a time, and beat until the spoonbread batter is smooth and creamy.

4 In a large bowl, beat the egg whites until they form stiff peaks. Fold them into the cornmeal mixture.

5 Pour the batter into a well-greased 1.5 litre/2½ pint/6¼ cup baking dish. Bake for 30–40 minutes until the bread is puffed and brown. Use a spoon to serve the bread. Hand round butter separately.

SPICED AUBERGINE FRIED IN CORNMEAL

T hese crisp aubergine slices are very good with plain grilled meat, poultry or fish. They can be served instead of meat in a vegetarian meal.

INGREDIENTS
1 large aubergine
salt
1 egg
120ml/4fl oz/½ cup milk
2.5ml/½ tsp paprika
2.5ml/½ tsp cayenne pepper
2.5ml/½ tsp ground black pepper
2.5ml/½ tsp garlic salt
115g/4oz/scant 1 cup fine cornmeal
oil for deep frying

SERVES 3–4

1 Cut the aubergine into 1cm/½in thick slices. Sprinkle lightly with salt and stack them in a colander. Leave standing in the sink to drain for 30 minutes, then wipe the slices dry on kitchen paper.

2 Beat the egg lightly in a shallow bowl with the milk, spices, pepper and garlic salt. Spread the cornmeal on a plate. Heat the oil for deep frying.

3 Dip each slice of aubergine in the spiced egg mixture, allowing the excess to drip back into the bowl. Turn the slice in the cornmeal; drop at once into the oil.

4 Fry three or four slices at a time, turning once, until they are golden on both sides. Drain on kitchen paper; keep warm until all the slices are fried. Serve hot.

BLACK-EYED BEAN SALAD

T his hearty, simple-to-make salad is served warm so that the flavours absorbed by the beans may be enjoyed at their fullest.

INGREDIENTS
2 small red peppers
2.5ml/½ tsp Dijon mustard
30ml/2 tbsp wine vinegar
1.5ml/¼ tsp salt
pinch of ground black pepper
90ml/6 tbsp olive oil
30ml/2 tbsp snipped fresh chives
425g/15oz can black-eyed beans
1 bay leaf
8 lean bacon rashers
flat leaf parsley, to garnish

SERVES 4

1 Preheat the grill. When hot, grill the peppers until the skins blacken and blister, turning them so that all sides are charred. Remove from the grill and seal in a paper bag. Leave for 10 minutes.

2 Peel off the skins. Cut the peppers in half, discard the seeds, white pith and stem, and slice into 1 x 5cm/½ x 2in strips. Set aside.

3 Combine the mustard and vinegar in a small bowl. Add the salt and pepper. Beat in the oil until well blended. Add the snipped fresh chives.

4 Drain and rinse the black-eyed beans. Heat the beans with the bay leaf for about 5 minutes, until just warmed through.

5 Meanwhile, cook the bacon until crisp. Drain on kitchen paper, then cut or break into small pieces.

6 Drain the beans and discard the bay leaf. While still warm, toss the beans with the chive dressing.

7 Make a mound of beans on a serving dish. Sprinkle with the bacon and serve, garnished with red pepper and parsley.

COOK'S TIP
If preferred, chop the peppers and mix into the warm beans at step 6.

POOR BOY STEAK SALAD

Poor Boy started life in the Italian Creole community of New Orleans when the poor survived on sandwiches filled with leftover scraps. Times have improved since then, and today the sandwich is commonly filled with tender beef steak and other goodies. This is a salad version of "Poor Boy".

INGREDIENTS
*4 sirloin or rump steaks, about
175g/6oz each
1 escarole lettuce
1 bunch watercress
4 tomatoes, quartered
4 large gherkins, sliced
4 spring onions, sliced
4 canned artichoke hearts, halved
175g/6oz button mushrooms, sliced
12 green olives
120ml/4fl oz/½ cup French dressing
salt and ground black pepper*

SERVES 4

1 Season the steaks with black pepper. Cook the steaks under a moderate grill for 6–8 minutes, turning once, until medium-rare. Cover and leave to rest in a warm place until needed.

2 Wash and dry the leaves. Combine with the rest of the ingredients (except the steak) and toss in the French dressing.

3 Divide the salad among four plates. Slice each steak diagonally and position over the salad. Season with salt and serve.

PECAN PIE

This is a favourite pie all over the southern states, where pecan nuts flourish. It is delicious served warm with cream or ice cream.

INGREDIENTS
FOR THE PASTRY
200g/7oz/1¾ cups plain flour
pinch of salt
115g/4oz/½ cup butter
iced water
dried beans or rice, for baking blind

FOR THE FILLING
3 eggs
good pinch of salt
5ml/1 tsp vanilla essence
200g/7oz/scant 1 cup well-packed soft
dark brown sugar
60ml/4 tbsp golden syrup or light
corn syrup
50g/2oz/4 tbsp butter, melted
115g/4oz/1 cup chopped pecan nuts, plus
12 pecan nut halves
whipped cream or vanilla ice cream,
to serve

SERVES 6

1 For the pastry, mix the flour with the salt, then rub in the butter with your fingertips to a coarse sand consistency. Add iced water a little at a time, mixing first with a fork, then with your hand, until the mixture gathers into a dough.

2 Wrap the dough in clear film and chill for 30–40 minutes. Preheat the oven to 190°C/375°F/Gas 5.

3 Grease a 20–23cm/8–9in loose-based flan tin. Roll out the pastry to line the tin, pressing it into place with your fingers.

COOK'S TIP
The corn syrup that American cooks use in their pie filling is not widely available outside the USA. You can find it in the larger department store food halls in major cities, or use golden syrup instead of corn syrup.

4 Run the rolling pin over the top of the tin to trim the surplus pastry, giving a neat finish to the pastry case.

5 Prick the pastry base with a fork and line with foil. Fill with dried beans or rice and bake blind for 15 minutes, then remove the foil and beans or rice and bake for a further 5 minutes. Take the pastry case from the oven and lower the oven temperature to 180°C/350°F/Gas 4.

6 Meanwhile, to make the filling, beat the eggs lightly with the salt and vanilla essence, then beat in the sugar, syrup and melted butter. Finally, mix in the chopped pecan nuts.

7 Spread the mixture in the half-baked pastry case and bake for 15 minutes, then take it from the oven and stud with the pecan nut halves in a circle.

8 Return to the oven and bake for a further 20–25 minutes until a thin metal skewer inserted gently into the centre comes out clean.

9 Cool the pie for 10–15 minutes and serve it warm with whipped cream or a scoop of vanilla ice cream. Any leftover pie may be served cold.

PRALINES

P ronounced with a long "a" and the stress on the first syllable, these resemble puddles of nut fudge more than the crisp biscuits Europeans think of as pralines. In Louisiana they are eaten as a dessert or whenever it seems a good idea to have something sweet with a cup of coffee.

INGREDIENTS
225g/8oz/2 cups pecan nut halves
450g/1lb/2 cups well-packed soft light brown sugar
200g/7oz/1 cup granulated sugar
300ml/½ pint/1¼ cups double cream
175ml/6fl oz/¾ cup milk
5ml/1 tsp vanilla essence

MAKES ABOUT 30 PIECES

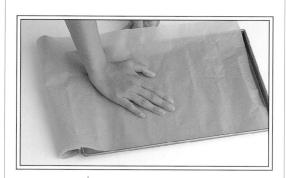

1 Roughly chop half the pecan nuts and set all the nuts aside. Line 2–3 baking sheets with non-stick baking paper.

2 Mix together the soft light brown sugar, granulated sugar, cream and milk in a saucepan over a moderate heat. Stir continuously until the mixture reaches 119°C/238°F on a sugar thermometer.

3 Remove from the heat immediately and beat with an electric beater or a balloon whisk until the mixture loses its sheen and becomes creamy in texture and grainy looking. This could take 15 minutes by hand or about 5 minutes with an electric beater.

4 Stir in the vanilla and nuts and drop large spoonfuls of the mixture on to the baking sheets. Leave to cool and set.

BANANAS FOSTER

A now-famous dessert named after Dick Foster, who was on the Vice Committee and therefore in charge of cleaning up the French Quarter of New Orleans in the 1950s.

INGREDIENTS
75g/3oz/¾ cup soft light brown sugar
2.5ml/½ tsp ground cinnamon
2.5ml/½ tsp grated nutmeg
50g/2oz/4 tbsp butter
60ml/4 tbsp banana liqueur
75ml/5 tbsp dark rum
4 firm bananas, peeled and halved lengthways
4 scoops firmly frozen vanilla ice cream, to serve

SERVES 4

1 Mix the sugar, cinnamon and nutmeg in a bowl. Melt the butter in a frying pan and add the sugar and spice mixture.

2 Add the liqueur and rum and stir over the heat until the sauce is syrupy.

3 Add the bananas and heat through, turning with a spoon to coat with the sauce.

4 If you are cooking over gas, tilt the pan to set light to the sauce. If your stove is electric, light the sauce with a match. Hold the pan at arm's length while you do this.

5 As soon as the flames die down, put pieces of banana on each plate with a scoop of ice cream. Pour on the sauce and serve immediately.

COOK'S TIP
You can ring the changes with praline or walnut ice creams.

MISSISSIPPI MUD CAKE

I f you do not have a bundt tin, an ordinary ring mould will do – it will not alter the glorious taste of this rich dessert!

INGREDIENTS
225g/8oz/2 cups plain flour
pinch of salt
5ml/1 tsp baking powder
300ml/½ pint/1¼ cups strong brewed coffee
50ml/2fl oz/¼ cup bourbon or brandy
150g/5oz plain chocolate
225g/8oz/1 cup butter or margarine
400g/14oz/2 cups granulated sugar
2 eggs, at room temperature
7.5ml/1½ tsp vanilla essence
cocoa powder for dusting
sweetened whipped cream or ice cream, to serve

SERVES 8–10

1 Preheat the oven to 140°C/275°F/Gas 1. Sift the flour, salt and baking powder together into a mixing bowl and set aside until required.

2 Combine the coffee, bourbon or brandy, chocolate and butter or margarine in the top of a double boiler or in a bowl set over a pan of simmering water. Heat until the chocolate and butter have melted and the mixture is smooth, stirring occasionally.

3 Pour the chocolate mixture into a large bowl. Using an electric mixer on low speed, gradually beat in the sugar. Continue beating until the sugar has dissolved.

4 Increase the speed to medium and add the sifted dry ingredients. Mix well, then beat in the eggs and vanilla until thoroughly blended and smooth.

5 Pour the mixture into a well-greased 3 litre/5 pint/12½ cup bundt tin that has been dusted lightly with cocoa powder. Bake for 1 hour 20 minutes in the oven until a skewer inserted in the cake comes out completely clean.

6 Leave the cake to cool in the bundt tin for about 15 minutes, then unmould it on to a wire rack and set aside until it is completely cooled.

7 When the cake is cold, dust it lightly with cocoa powder. Serve with sweetened whipped cream or ice cream, if desired. Use vanilla, or other flavoured ice creams if you prefer.

CORNMEAL SCONES

For a morning snack or a tea-time treat there is nothing better than scones, hot from the oven and spread with plenty of butter.

INGREDIENTS

150g/5oz/1¼ cups plain flour
12.5ml/2½ tsp baking powder
4.5ml/¾ tsp salt
60g/2¼oz/½ cup cornmeal, plus more for sprinkling
65g/2½oz/5 tbsp white vegetable fat or cold butter
175ml/6fl oz/¾ cup milk
butter or margarine, to serve

MAKES ABOUT 12

1 Preheat the oven to 230°C/450°F/Gas 8. Sift the dry ingredients. Stir in the cornmeal. Rub in the fat or butter until the mixture resembles coarse meal.

2 Make a well in the centre and pour in the milk. Stir in quickly with a wooden spoon for 1 minute, until the dough begins to pull away from the sides of the bowl.

3 Turn the dough on to a lightly floured surface and knead lightly 8–10 times only. Roll out to a thickness of 1cm/½in. Cut into rounds with a floured 5cm/2in biscuit cutter. Do not twist the cutter.

4 Sprinkle an ungreased baking sheet lightly with cornmeal. Arrange the scones on the sheet, about 2.5cm/1in apart. Sprinkle the scones with more cornmeal.

5 Bake until golden brown, for about 10–12 minutes. Serve the scones hot, with butter or margarine.

FRENCH QUARTER BEIGNETS

T hese lightly spiced, deep fried fritters are so easy to make and welcome at any time of day, with a sprinkling of icing sugar.

INGREDIENTS
225g/8oz/2 cups plain flour
5ml/1 tsp salt
15ml/1 tbsp baking powder
5ml/1 tsp ground cinnamon
2 eggs
50g/2oz/¼ cup granulated sugar
175ml/6fl oz/¾ cup milk
2.5ml/½ tsp vanilla essence
oil for deep frying
icing sugar, for sprinkling

MAKES ABOUT 20

1 To make the dough, sift the flour, salt, baking powder and ground cinnamon into a large mixing bowl. Cover and set aside until required.

2 In a separate bowl, beat together the eggs, granulated sugar, milk and vanilla essence. Mix this into the flour mixture to form a dough.

3 Turn the dough on to a lightly floured surface and knead until smooth and elastic. Roll it out to a round 5mm/¼in thick. Slice diagonally into diamonds about 7.5cm/3in long.

4 Heat oil in a deep fryer or large, heavy-based saucepan to 190°C/375°F. Fry the beignets in the oil, a few at a time, turning once, until golden brown. Remove with a slotted spoon and drain well on kitchen paper. Before serving, sprinkle the beignets with icing sugar.

PECAN NUT DIVINITY CAKE

This three-layered cake, with its meringue-style icing, tastes truly heavenly. It looks impressive but is surprisingly simple to make.

INGREDIENTS
275g/10oz/2½ cups pecan nuts
350g/12oz/3 cups plain flour
7.5ml/1½ tsp baking powder
2.5ml/½ tsp salt
225g/8oz/1 cup unsalted butter, at room temperature
400g/14oz/2 cups caster sugar
5 eggs
250ml/8fl oz/1 cup milk
5ml/1 tsp vanilla essence

FOR THE DIVINITY ICING
350g/12oz/3 cups icing sugar
3 egg whites, at room temperature
2 drops vanilla essence

SERVES 6–8

1 Toast the pecan nuts in batches in a heavy-based pan over a high heat, tossing regularly until they darken and give off a toasted aroma. Cool, then chop the nuts coarsely.

2 Preheat the oven to 180°C/350°F/Gas 4. Oil and lightly flour three 23cm/9in round cake tins. Sift the flour, baking powder and salt together. Toss half the pecan nuts in 30ml/2 tbsp of the flour mixture. Reserve the remaining nuts for the final decoration.

3 Cream the butter and sugar until pale and fluffy and add the eggs, one at a time, beating well after each addition.

4 Mix the milk with the vanilla essence. Stir the flour into the creamed mixture in three batches, alternating with the milk. Finally fold in the floured nuts.

5 Pour the cake mixture into the prepared tins and bake in the oven for 30 minutes, until the tops are golden brown and the cakes have shrunk from the side of the tins. Cool in the tins for 5 minutes before turning out on to wire racks to cool completely.

6 To make the icing, sift the icing sugar into a bowl, add the egg whites and set the bowl over a pan of boiling water. Whisk for 5–10 minutes until stiff peaks form.

7 Add the vanilla. Remove the bowl from the pan and whisk for 2–3 minutes. Sandwich the cake layers with some icing, sprinkling each layer with some reserved pecan nuts.

8 Ice the top and sides of the assembled cake and sprinkle the remaining nuts on top to finish.

INDEX